Rookie
Read-About® Geography

Vermont

By Christine Taylor-Butler

Subject Consultant
Amy Cunningham
Director of Education
Vermont Historical Society
Barre, Vermont

Reading Consultant
Cecilia Minden-Cupp, PhD
Former Director of the Language and Literacy Program
Harvard Graduate School of Education
Cambridge, Massachusetts

Children's Press®
A Division of Scholastic Inc.
New York   Toronto   London   Auckland   Sydney
Mexico City   New Delhi   Hong Kong
Danbury, Connecticut

Designer: Herman Adler
Photo Researcher: Caroline Anderson
The photo on the cover shows a country road leading to a
Vermont farmhouse.

Library of Congress Cataloging-in-Publication Data

Taylor-Butler, Christine.
  Vermont / by Christine Taylor-Butler.
      p. cm. — (Rookie read-about geography)
  Includes index.
  ISBN-13: 978-0-531-12593-9 (lib. bdg.)   978-0-531-16819-6 (pbk.)
  ISBN-10: 0-531-12593-9 (lib. bdg.)   0-531-16819-0 (pbk.)
  1. Vermont—Juvenile literature. 2. Vermont—Geography—Juvenile
literature. I. Title. II. Series.
  F49.3.T39 2007
  974.3—dc22   2006017611

Do you know why Vermont is called the Green Mountain State?

Vermont has many mountains covered with trees. *Verts monts* is French for "green mountains."

Can you find Vermont on this map?

Fall in Vermont

Many people visit Vermont
to enjoy the scenery.
In fall, the trees are
covered with beautiful
orange, yellow, and
red leaves.

Vermont's state tree is the sugar maple. The sap, or liquid, from this tree is used to make maple syrup.

Sap from a sugar maple collects in a bucket.

A hermit thrush

Vermont's state bird is the hermit thrush.

The state flower is the red clover.

The Northeast Highlands is a region, or section, in northeastern Vermont.

This region is filled with many forests. Black bears, moose, and beavers live in the Northeast Highlands.

A black bear

This Vermont quarry contains granite.

The Vermont Piedmont is a region in eastern Vermont. This area has mountains that are made from a rock called granite.

The Vermont Piedmont is also filled with lakes, ponds, and swamps.

Mount Mansfield is the highest point in Vermont. It rises more than 4,000 feet (1,200 meters)!

Mount Mansfield is part of the Green Mountain Region in central Vermont.

Mount Mansfield rises behind a Vermont farmhouse.

A bat

The Taconic Mountains
in southwestern Vermont
have many underground
rivers and caves. Bats spend
time in these caves during
the winter.

The Champlain Valley is
a region in northwestern
Vermont.

Farmers in this area
grow apples, corn,
oats, and wheat.

A Vermont cornfield

21

Lake Champlain

Vermont shares Lake Champlain with New York and Canada.

Fish such as pike, walleye, and trout live in the lake. In the winter, Lake Champlain freezes, and people go ice fishing.

The capital of Vermont is Montpelier.

Burlington is Vermont's largest city.

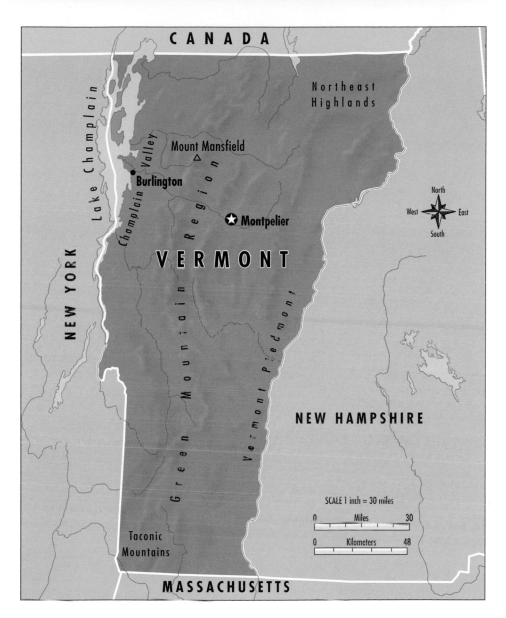

CANADA

Northeast
Highlands

Lake Champlain

Champlain Valley

Mount Mansfield
△

● Burlington

★ Montpelier

VERMONT

NEW YORK

Green Mountain Region

Vermont Piedmont

North
West ✦ East
South

NEW HAMPSHIRE

Taconic
Mountains

SCALE 1 inch = 30 miles

0   Miles   30

0   Kilometers   48

MASSACHUSETTS

Skiing in Vermont

People who live in
Vermont have many jobs.
Some own farms and raise
cows for their milk.

Other people work with
visitors to the state.
Vermont is a popular
place for skiers. They
enjoy racing down the
snowy mountainsides.

Maybe one day you will visit Vermont.

What will you do first when you get there?

Visitors enjoy a camping trip in Vermont.

Words You Know

black bear

corn

granite

hermit thrush

30

Lake Champlain

Mount Mansfield

sap

skier

31

Index

About the Author

Christine Taylor-Butler is the author of twenty-eight books for children and is a native of Ohio. She is a graduate of the Massachusetts Institute of Technology and is also the author of five other books in the Rookie Reader Read-About® Geography series: *Hawaii, Kansas, Missouri, The Missouri River,* and *Ohio.*

Photo Credits

Photographs © 2007: Alamy Images/Dennis Hallinan: 3; Aurora Photos/David McLain: 26, 31 bottom right; Corbis Images: 22, 31 top left (James P. Blair), 13, 30 top left (Daniel J. Cox), 6 (Peter Finger), 18 (Joe McDonald), 29 (Royalty-Free), 14, 30 bottom left (Joseph Sohm); Getty Images/Ron & Patty Thomas/Taxi: cover; Minden Pictures/Tom Vezo: 10, 30 bottom right; photolibrary.com/Oxford Scientific/Foodpix: 21, 30 top right; The Image Works/Andre Jenny: 17, 31 top right; Visuals Unlimited/John Sohldon: 9, 31 bottom left.

Maps by Bob Italiano